Better BARBECUES

'Food always tastes better when eaten out of doors.' There's a lot of truth in the old adage – there's no finer stimulus to appetite than the aroma of succulent steak, sizzling on the barbecue grill – and lying back in a garden chair with a drink at your elbow and the relaxing company of close friends is one of the better aids to digestion.

Of course, barbecues aren't always hassle free. We've all know occasions when the charcoal wouldn't burn, the weather failed to come up to expectations, the jacket potatoes were not cooked on time and the fire wasn't the only thing that flared up; but that's part and parcel of the barbecue experience. Most pitfalls – barring tempests, torrential rain or fire bans – can be avoided by careful planning. The opening chapter of this book, Barbecue Know-how, offers advice from the experts.

The recipes that follow range from fragrant fish kebabs to hearty hamburgers. Marinades and sauces are used to good advantage, and there are plenty of suggestions for out-of-the-ordinary dishes like Quails with Soy Honey Glaze and Raspberry Marinated Chicken Wings. Salads and Side dishes have been selected to offer vegetarians viable alternatives. This is often preferable to simply cooking a vegetable kebab or stuffed pepper alongside the meat, which can lead to an unacceptable transfer of fats and flavours.

CONTENTS

BARBEQUE KNOW-HOW

There are few meals more enjoyable than a relaxing barbecue – and few culinary experiences more catastrophic than the cookout that turns into a flaming disaster. So how do you plan the perfect al fresco meal?

The Site

Whether your barbecue is a handy hibachi, a convenient kettle or a thing of brick-built beauty that is your partner's pride and joy, the site for your fire is all important. It should be close to the kitchen, in as sheltered a position as possible, but away from obvious hazards like overhanging branches or adjacent bushes. If you are new to barbecuing it is a good idea to begin with a small portable barbecue: that way you can experiment with various sites until you find the place that is as near perfect as wind and weather will permit.

Planning

The best barbecue cooks get organised in plenty of time: laying in stocks of charcoal, hickory chips and firelighters; making special marinades and sauces; making sure all necessary tools, including turners and tongs, are to hand, and remembering not only the matches for starting the fire, but also a water pistol for dousing unwanted flames and flare-ups.

Fuel

Both gas and electric barbecues are available, but by far the most frequently used form of fuel is charcoal, either in lump form or as briquettes. Briquettes are more expensive than lump charcoal, but generally burn for longer.

Whichever form you choose, one of the simplest ways of laying a fire is to mound the charcoal in a pyramid in the centre of your firebox, inserting solid firelighters between the coals. Alternatively –

and this is really easy – buy instant-burning briquettes in a bag that fits your barbecue. All you do is light the bag; the fire will be ready in twenty minutes.

Cooking

As with other forms of cooking, practice makes perfect. Impatience is a common fault. Most fires should be lit at least 45 minutes before cooking is to commence; briquettes are ready when they are ash-grey all over, with glowing hearts. Only then should the coals be spread out for cooking; close together (but not a solid mass) for intense, concentrated heat; spread out for more gentle heat over a wider area. When using a rotisserie, or when cooking joints, it is usual to cook by indirect heat; either arranging the coals in a ring or placing them towards the back of the barbecue. A tin may be placed under the joint to catch the juices.

Most barbecues have grills whose height above the fire can be adjusted. Other ways of controlling the degree of heat include changing the shape of the fire, adding or subtracting fuel and using a windbreak.

The food

A wide range of foods can be successfully cooked on the barbecue, including fish, meats (steaks, chops, sausages, burgers, kebabs – even whole joints), vegetables and fruit.

Fish

Fish is one of the great successes of the barbecue story, but like the

girl with the curl, when it is good it is very very good, but when it is bad it is horrid. The secret is in the selection (choose firm fish for cooking directly over the coals; wrap the more delicate varieties in foil); the saucing (use marinades by all means, but make sure they are in keeping with the flavour of the fish) and in sensitive heat control. Fish should be cooked by moderate, not fierce heat, so either allow the initial heat of the coals to subside somewhat, or raise the grill. Crisp, lightly charred skin improves the flavour of oily fish like sardines; move them nearer the heat source for the final few minutes of cooking if liked, but take care not to overcook.

Even over relatively gentle heat, fish cooks swiftly. If cooking a whole fish, slash the skin in several places, through to the bone, to conduct the heat efficiently. Check frequently and remove the fish from the heat source as soon as the flesh flakes readily when tested with the tip of a knife. The flesh of even the more robust varieties is delicate, so take particular care when turning fish; hinged grills are an inexpensive and highly successful solution to the problem, but, as with any surface with which the fish comes into contact, they must be well oiled before use. If cooking whole fish, place the tail ends towards the hinge.

Cooking with Herbs

The wonderful aroma of fresh herbs is entirely in keeping with the outdoor aspect of barbecue

Mixed Seafood Skewers (page 5), cooked to perfection on the barbecue

cookery. Add finely chopped parsley, tarragon, chervil or chives to foil parcels; make fresh herb stuffings, thread bay leaves on kebab skewers or simply strew fresh dill, rosemary, thyme or fennel directly onto the coals towards the end of cooking.

Poultry
Poultry tastes delicious when cooked on the barbecue. Chicken wings, with plum sauce or marinated in raspberry vinegar and oil, make an inexpensive and tasty meal for all the family. Simply add jacket potatoes and a salad. Chicken quarters and drumsticks are also ideal barbecue candidates, but take care that breasts do not overcook. Don't forget game birds when planning a barbecue feast – quail is an excellent choice.

Meat
Flares might find favour in fashion, but in culinary terms they are most definitely to be avoided. The aim is to cook by controlled heat, charring the meat but avoiding the burnt offerings that result from sudden gouts of flame caused by fat dripping on the coals. Always trim excess fat from meats, especially lamb and pork, and use good quality low fat minced beef for burgers.

Vegetables and Fruit
Courgettes can be cooked whole on the barbecue, or share a skewer with tomatoes, peppers, aubergine cubes and mushrooms for a vegetarian treat. For a simple taste sensation, cook matchsticks of root vegetables (carrots, parsnips, swedes) in foil parcels with a knob of butter and a sprinkling of fresh herbs,

As for fruit, banana and pineapple have a special affinity for fireside meals; try the recipe for barbecued bananas in this book.

Microwave Magic
The microwave is a wonderful aid to better barbecuing. Items such as chicken drumsticks or thighs can be partially cooked in the microwave before being finished off on the barbecue grill, thus ensuring that the poultry is perfectly cooked all the way through - and saving both time and energy.

Sausages can be given the same treatment, but items such as chicken breasts and steaks, which cook quickly over hot coals, should not be precooked.

Safety first and last
Always take care when cooking on the barbecue. Ensure that children and animals are kept well away from the area, use long, preferably wooden-handled tools, never leave a fire unattended and smother the fire after cooking.

FISH AL FRESCO

Although meat comes to mind most readily when barbecues are mentioned, fish is rapidly moving up to first place in the popularity stakes. The flavour of fish cooked over coals is unbeatable, provided the flesh remains moist and the delicate flavours are not dominated by strident sauces. Follow the suggestions in Barbecue Know-how for perfect results every time.

Fish Kebabs with Sesame Sauce

500g (1lb) firm white fish fillets, cut into 2cm (³/4in) cubes

2 cloves garlic, crushed

60ml (2fl oz) freshly squeezed lime juice

3 tblspn sesame seeds

60ml (2fl oz) olive oil

250g (8oz) cherry tomatoes

Sesame Sauce

45g (1¹/2oz) butter

1 onion, finely chopped

1 tspn ground cumin

1 tspn ground coriander

60ml (2fl oz) sweet sherry

3 tblspn tahini

1 tblspn honey

2 tblspn peanut butter

1 tblspn freshly squeezed lime juice

60ml (2fl oz) water

1 Spread out fish cubes in a single layer in a large shallow dish. Mix garlic, lime juice, sesame seeds and oil in a bowl. Pour mixture over fish, cover dish and set aside to marinate for 30 minutes.

2 Make sauce. Melt butter in a medium saucepan over moderate heat. Add onion and fry for 2 minutes, then stir in cumin and coriander and cook for 1 minute more.

3 Add sherry, tahini, honey, peanut butter, lime juice and water to sauce. Cook for 5 minutes, stirring constantly, until sauce thickens. Keep hot at the side of the barbecue.

4 Thread the fish and tomatoes alternately onto oiled metal or soaked wooden skewers. Grill over moderately hot coals until tender. Serve with the sauce.

Serves 4

Mixed Seafood Skewers

Illustrated on page 3

12 scallops, rinsed and deveined

12 uncooked king prawns, peeled and deveined, tails intact

2 firm fish fillets, cut into 2cm (³/4in) cubes

60g (2oz) butter

3 tblspn lemon juice

1 clove garlic, crushed

¹/4 tspn freshly ground black pepper

2 tblspn each chopped fresh chervil, dill and thyme

1 Keeping the types of seafood separate, thread the scallops, prawns and fish cubes onto 12 small oiled metal or soaked wooden skewers.

2 Melt the butter in a small saucepan. Stir in the lemon juice, garlic and pepper. Brush each kebab generously with the mixture. Sprinkle chervil over the scallops, dill over the prawns and thyme over the fish cubes.

3 Grill the kebabs over moderately hot coals for about 2 minutes each side or until tender.

Serves 4

Swordfish Steaks with Vegetable Ragout

90ml (3fl oz) olive oil

2 onions, thinly sliced

1 aubergine, cubed

1 small green pepper, sliced

1 small red pepper, sliced

1 fennel bulb, white part only, sliced

60ml (2fl oz) chicken stock

2 tblspn white wine vinegar

1 tblspn chopped fresh parsley

2 tspn chopped fresh oregano

2 cloves garlic, crushed

freshly ground black pepper

4 swordfish steaks

2 tblspn lemon juice

1 Heat 2 tablespoons of the oil in a large frying pan. Add the onion and cook, stirring, until brown. Add the aubergine cubes and fry lightly for 2 minutes, then stir in the peppers, fennel and stock. Bring to the boil, then simmer until the vegetables are tender.

2 Combine the remaining oil, vinegar, herbs and garlic in a screwtop jar. Close the lid tightly and shake well. Add pepper to taste. Pour half this dressing over the vegetable mixture; keep warm over low heat.

3 Grill the swordfish steaks over moderately hot coals until tender. Serve each steak on a bed of vegetable ragout. Sprinkle with the lemon juice and offer the remaining dressing separately.

Serves 4

Fish Kebabs with Sesame Sauce

Tuna with Herbed Tomato, Garlic and Lemon Sauce

2 tuna steaks, 3cm (1¼in) thick, about 500g (1lb) each

Sauce

750g (1½lb) tomatoes, peeled, seeded and finely chopped

125ml (4fl oz) olive oil

60ml (2fl oz) lemon juice

4 cloves garlic, crushed

salt

4 tblspn finely chopped mixed fresh herbs

1 Make the sauce. Combine the tomatoes, oil, lemon juice and garlic in a bowl. Add salt to taste. Cover the bowl and set aside for 2 hours at room temperature to allow the flavours to blend.

2 Grill the tuna steaks over moderately hot coals until cooked to your taste, turning once. Slice the fish into thick strips and arrange on a platter.

3 Stir the fresh herbs into the tomato sauce; pour half the mixture over the tuna strips and serve the rest separately.

Serves 6

Sea Bream Kebabs with Apple Marinade

185ml (6fl oz) apple juice

2 tspn ground cumin

2 tspn grated fresh root ginger

2 cloves garlic, crushed

1 red chilli, seeded and chopped

750g (1½lb) sea bream or other firm fish fillets, cut into 3cm (1¼in) cubes

1 cucumber

1 x 375g (12oz) can pineapple rings, drained

1 Combine apple juice, cumin, ginger, garlic and chilli in a shallow dish, large enough to hold all the fish cubes in a single layer. Add fish, turning cubes over in marinade. Cover; set aside for 1 hour.

2 Cut cucumber in half length-wise; scoop out seeds. Cut flesh into chunks, the same size as the fish. Cut each pineapple ring into three wedges.

3 Drain fish, reserving marinade. Thread fish, cucumber and pineapple alternately onto oiled metal skewers. Brush with marinade. Grill over moderately hot coals until tender, basting frequently with marinade.

Serves 4

Whiting with Sweet and Sour Rice

4 small whole whiting, cleaned and scaled

2 tblspn lemon juice

2 tblspn olive oil, plus extra for foil

Rice

60ml (2fl oz) sunflower or olive oil

1 large onion, chopped

30g (1oz) pinenuts

185g (6oz) long-grain rice

1 tblspn grated root ginger

½ red pepper, finely chopped

4 baby corn cobs, sliced

500ml (16fl oz) water

2 tblspn sugar

2 tblspn lemon juice

1 tblspn chopped fresh parsley

1 Prepare the rice. Heat the sunflower oil in a large frying pan, add the onion and pinenuts and cook for 2 minutes.

2 Stir in rice, ginger, red pepper and corn. Cook for 1 minute, then add water. Bring to boil, lower heat and simmer for 15 minutes, until the rice is tender and water has evaporated. (Add more water if necessary.) Stir in sugar and lemon juice and cook for 2 minutes more. Keep the rice hot.

3 Wash fish and season it inside and out. Mix lemon juice and olive oil together in a cup; brush mixture over outside of each fish. Wrap fish in oiled heavy duty foil; cook on a grill over moderately hot coals for about 30 minutes or until tender.

4 Stir the parsley into the rice and divide it between four plates. Remove the fish from the foil and place on top of the rice. Serve.

Serves 4

Whiting with Sweet and Sour Rice

Baked Snapper with Artichoke Stuffing

30g (1oz) butter, plus extra for foil

1 onion, chopped

2 cloves garlic, crushed

1/2 red pepper, chopped

5 drained canned artichoke hearts, finely chopped

1 tblspn chopped fresh parsley

30g (1oz) dried breadcrumbs

5 tblspn freshly squeezed lime juice

2 snapper or red mullet, cleaned, head and tail left on

2 tblspn lemon juice

60ml (2fl oz) dry white wine

coriander sprig for garnish

1 Melt butter in a medium frying pan over moderate heat. Add onion, garlic and red pepper; fry for 3-4 minutes until softened. Stir in artichokes, parsley and bread-crumbs. Moisten with 2 table-spoons of lime juice. Fill each fish cavity with artichoke stuffing.

2 Generously butter two sheets of foil, each large enough to enclose one of the fish. Mix the remaining lime juice with the lemon juice and white wine.

3 Place a fish on each piece of foil, taking care not to spill the stuffing. Bring up the sides of the foil slightly to form a lip. Pour half the wine mixture over each fish, then bring up the sides of the foil completely to enclose each fish in a loose parcel.

4 Barbecue over moderately hot coals until the fish is cooked through. Serve immediately, garnished with coriander.
Serves 4

Baked Snapper with Artichoke Stuffing, Scallop and Prawn Kebabs with Mango Marinade

Scallop and Prawn Kebabs with Mango Marinade

You will need 12 wooden skewers to make these kebabs. Soak them in warm water for 1 hour before use to prevent scorching.

1 large mango, peeled and chopped, flesh chopped

2 tblspn freshly squeezed lime juice

18 scallops, rinsed and deveined

18 uncooked king prawns, peeled and deveined, tails intact

1/2 tspn crushed black peppercorns

1 christophene or choko or 4 courgettes, cut into 2cm (3/4in) cubes

1 Combine the mango and lime juice in a blender or food processor. Process until smooth; scrape the purée into a large bowl.

2 Add the scallops, prawns and crushed peppercorns to the bowl. Stir to coat the seafood in the mango purée, then cover and refrigerate for 1 hour.

3 Bring a large saucepan of water to the boil, add the christophene or choko pieces and cook for 4 minutes. Drain, refresh under cold water and drain again. There is no need to blanch the courgettes.

4 Thread the scallops, prawns and christophene, choko or courgette pieces on the drained wooden skewers.

5 Brush with the mango marinade. Cook over medium coals for 1-2 minutes on each side. Serve.

Serves 4

Grilled Marinated Cod

250ml (8fl oz) hoisin sauce

125ml (4fl oz) dry vermouth

45g (1¹/₂oz) sugar

6 cod cutlets, each 2cm (³/₄in) thick

60g (2oz) butter, melted

2 tblspn finely chopped spring onion

2 tblspn lemon juice

coriander sprigs for garnish

1 Combine hoisin sauce, vermouth and sugar.

2 Place cod cutlets in a dish in a single layer. Pour hoisin mixture over, cover dish and refrigerate for at least 8 hours, turning from time to time.

3 Combine butter, spring onion and lemon juice. Place cutlets in a hinged grill; brush generously with butter mixture.

4 Cook cutlets over medium coals until tender, brushing frequently with butter mixture. Serve garnished with coriander sprigs.

Serves 6

Barbecued Spiced Swordfish

4 swordfish steaks

2 tblspn Worcestershire sauce

2 tblspn sunflower oil

2 tspn soy sauce

¹/₂ tspn chilli powder

2 cloves garlic, crushed

Tabasco sauce to taste

1 Arrange swordfish steaks in a dish large enough to hold them in a single layer.

2 Mix remaining ingredients in a small bowl; pour over the swordfish, cover and set aside for 1 hour.

3 Cook swordfish over moderately hot coals, basting frequently with marinade, until tender.

Serves 4

Salmon with Lime Butter Baste

90g (3oz) butter

1 clove garlic, crushed

60ml (2fl oz) freshly squeezed lime juice

2 tspn grated lime rind

2 tspn grated lemon rind

1 tblspn dry white wine

2 tspn honey

1 tblspn chopped fresh parsley

4 x 200g (6¹/₂oz) salmon or other firm fish fillets

1 Melt the butter in a small saucepan over moderate heat. Stir in the garlic and cook for 1 minute. Add the lime juice, lime rind, lemon rind, wine and honey; mix well. Stir in the parsley.

2 Cook the salmon fillets over moderately hot coals, brushing frequently with the lime butter baste, for about 3 minutes on each side or until cooked through.

Serves 4

Barbecued Prawns

Prawns are easily overcooked. Do not place them too close to the coals, and remove them from the heat as soon as they are tender.

500g (1lb) uncooked king prawns, peeled and deveined, tails intact

2 tspn sesame oil, plus extra for skewers

1 tblspn rich soy sauce

1 tblspn oil

1 tspn honey

1 clove garlic, crushed

1 Thread prawns onto oiled metal skewers. Mix the remaining ingredients in a small bowl. Using a brush, generously 'paint' the prawns with sesame oil mixture.

2 Cook prawn kebabs over moderately hot coals, turning once, until tender. Brush frequently with remaining sesame oil mixture.

Serves 4

Broad Bean and Tomato Salad (page 34), Salmon with Lime Butter Baste

Grilled Mustard Cutlets

2 tblspn grainy mustard

1 tblspn honey

60ml (2fl oz) dry white wine

1 clove garlic, crushed

4 x 185g (6oz) fish cutlets

1 Combine mustard, honey, wine and garlic in a shallow bowl. Mix well. Turn the cutlets in the mixture until coated on both sides. Set aside for 30 minutes.

2 Cook the fish over moderately hot coals until tender.

Serves 4

Orange Fish Parcels

2 tspn olive oil

1 tspn grated orange rind

60ml (2fl oz) orange juice

1 tspn chopped fresh dill

1 tblspn snipped fresh chives

1/2 tspn soy sauce

4 x 185g (6oz) white fish fillets, skinned

1 Generously brush with oil four squares of foil, each large enough to enclose one of the fish fillets.

2 Combine the orange rind, orange juice, dill, chives and soy sauce in a small bowl.

3 Place a fish fillet on each foil square; sprinkle with the orange mixture. Bring up the sides of the foil to enclose each fish fillet in a loose parcel.

4 Place the fish parcels directly on the barbecue grill and cook until tender. To serve, place a foil parcel on each plate and carefully open the foil to reveal the fish.

Serves 4

Kitchen Tip
The cooking time for the fish parcels will depend upon the heat of the coals and the distance of the grill from the heat source; when the flesh flakes easily when tested with the tip of a sharp knife, it is ready.

Grilled Tuna with Green Peppercorns

Tuna steaks resemble beef steaks in that they are usually cooked to personal preference and may be served 'rare' – crisp on the outside but barely cooked within. Consult your guests before grilling the fish.

4 x 155g (5oz) tuna steaks

freshly ground black pepper

2 tblspn chopped fresh parsley

Sauce

125ml (4fl oz) dry white wine

juice of 1 lemon

1 tblspn finely chopped onion

15g (1/2oz) butter

1 tblspn green peppercorns

1 Season tuna steaks generously with pepper. Set aside.

2 Make sauce. Combine wine, lemon juice and onion in a small saucepan. Bring to the boil over moderate heat. Continue boiling until reduced by half.

3 Meanwhile, cook tuna steaks over moderately hot coals until done to your taste.

4 Whisk butter and peppercorns into the reduced sauce. Serve tuna steaks on heated plates, with sauce spooned over top. Garnish with the parsley.

Serves 4

Kitchen Tip
This recipe may be made using pink peppercorns, but these should be treated with caution, as they can provoke a violent allergic reaction in susceptible individuals.

Seafood Kebabs

Oregano Sardines

1kg (2lb) fresh sardines, heads removed, cleaned

125ml (4fl oz) olive oil

3 tblspn chopped fresh parsley

2 cloves garlic, crushed

1/2 tspn dried oregano

2 tblspn red wine vinegar

1 Split sardines open down the belly. Turn them over on a board, press down firmly on spines, then turn them over again; bones will come away easily. Rinse fish and pat dry with paper towels.

2 Combine all the remaining ingredients in a small bowl; mix well. Brush sardines generously with the oil mixture. Cook over moderately hot coals, brushing with oil mixture, until tender.

Serves 4

Sea Bass Fillets with Avocado Sauce

4 x 185g (6oz) sea bass fillets

5 tblspn olive oil

5 tblspn freshly squeezed lime juice

1 avocado, halved, stoned, peeled and cut into 5mm (1/4in) cubes

1 bunch chives, snipped

salt

freshly ground black pepper

1 Arrange fillets in a single layer in a dish. Brush with 1 tablespoon of oil. Drizzle 3 table-spoons of the lime juice over top. Cover dish and set aside for 15 minutes.

2 Combine avocado, remaining oil, remaining lime juice, chives and salt and pepper to taste.

3 Grill fillets, without turning, over moderately hot coals until cooked. Serve with avocado sauce.

Serves 4

Lime and Basil Grilled John Dory

500g (1lb) John Dory fillets

125ml (4fl oz) freshly squeezed lime juice

125ml (4fl oz) lemon juice

1 tblspn chopped fresh basil

1 tblspn snipped fresh chives

freshly ground black pepper

1 Arrange fillets in a shallow dish. Mix the citrus juices, herbs and pepper together and pour over fish, cover; set aside for 30 minutes.

2 Grill fillets, without turning, over moderately hot coals until cooked. Baste frequently with the marinade.

Serves 4

Seafood Kebabs

16 mangetout, trimmed

60g (2oz) butter, melted

3 tblspn freshly squeezed lime juice

1 tblspn finely chopped fresh mint

2 tblspn finely grated Parmesan cheese

16 scallops, rinsed and deveined

16 uncooked king prawns, peeled and deveined, tails intact

oil for greasing

1 Soak 8 wooden skewers in warm water for 1 hour. Blanch mangetout in boiling water, then drain and refresh under cold water. Drain again.

2 Combine butter, lime juice, mint and Parmesan cheese.

3 Wrap each scallop in a mangetout. Thread two prawns and two mangetout-wrapped scallops onto each drained skewer.

4 Brush kebabs generously with butter mixture. Barbecue on an oiled grill over moderately hot coals for 2 minutes each side or until tender, brushing with the butter mixture.

Serves 4

11

Cooked simply with a butter glaze, or dressed to impress with a spicy marinade or baste, perfectly char-grilled chicken, duck or game birds are crisp on the outside, tender and juicy within.

Spicy Chicken Satay with Peanut Sauce

6 chicken breast fillets

2 onions, chopped

2 cloves garlic, crushed

1 tblspn very finely chopped lemon grass

1 tspn ground coriander

1 tspn ground cumin

2 tspn grated fresh root ginger

60ml (2fl oz) oil

Peanut Sauce

1 onion, chopped

6 red chillies, chopped

125g (4oz) peanuts

60ml (2fl oz) oil

1 tblspn tamarind sauce

175ml (6fl oz) water

1 Cut the chicken into cubes; arrange in a single layer in a shallow bowl. Combine the onions, garlic, lemon grass, spices and oil in a blender or food processor; process until smooth. Pour over the chicken, stir to coat, then cover and refrigerate for 4-8 hours.

2 Drain the chicken cubes, discarding marinade. Thread cubes onto oiled metal or soaked wooden skewers; set aside.

3 Make sauce. Combine onion, chillies and peanuts in a blender or food processor; process until smooth. Heat oil in a sauce-pan, add onion mixture and cook, stirring, for 5 minutes. Add the tamarind sauce and water and bring to boil. Lower heat and simmer until sauce has reduced and thickened.

4 Cook the chicken over hot coals until tender and golden brown. Serve with the peanut sauce.

Serves 8

Raspberry Marinated Chicken Wings

24 chicken wings

Raspberry Marinade

250ml (8fl oz) olive oil

5 tblspn raspberry vinegar

1 tblspn honey

1 tblspn sesame seeds

1 tspn ground cumin

1/2 tspn salt

2 cloves garlic, crushed

1 Combine oil, vinegar, honey, sesame seeds, cumin, salt and garlic in a shallow dish, large enough to hold all chicken wings in a single layer. Mix well. Add chicken wings, stir to coat, then cover and refrigerate overnight.

2 Drain the chicken, reserving the marinade. Grill over hot coals until crisp and cooked through, basting occasionally with the marinade.

Serves 6-8

Spicy Chicken Satay with Peanut Sauce

Chicken Wings with Plum Sauce, Redcurrant Glazed Poussins

Rosemary Chicken Skewers

4 chicken breast fillets, cut into 2.5cm (1in) cubes

2 large onions, cut into eighths

Rosemary Marinade

125ml (4fl oz) olive oil

1 tblspn finely chopped garlic

1 tblspn chopped fresh rosemary

freshly ground black pepper

125ml (4fl oz) lemon juice

1 Whisk marinade ingredients together. Place chicken cubes in a single layer in a dish. Add onions. Add marinade, toss to coat. Cover and refrigerate for at least 8 hours, stirring occasionally.

2 Thread chicken and onion onto oiled metal skewers. Grill over hot coals until browned and tender, basting frequently with marinade.

Serves 4-8

Chicken Wings with Plum Sauce

125ml (4fl oz) plum sauce

125ml (4fl oz) soy sauce

60ml (2fl oz) red wine vinegar

1 clove garlic, crushed

1 tblspn grated fresh root ginger

16 chicken wings

3 tblspn sesame seeds

1 Combine plum sauce, soy sauce, vinegar, garlic and ginger.

2 Arrange chicken wings in a single layer in a shallow dish. Pour over sauce and stir to coat. Cover dish and refrigerate for at least 6 hours, preferably overnight.

3 Preheat oven to 180°C (350°F/ Gas 4). Place chicken and marinade in a roasting tin and cook for 30 minutes, turning once. Transfer chicken to an oiled barbecue grill. Brush with remaining marinade and sprinkle with sesame seeds. Barbecue for 5-10 minutes or until crisp and browned. Serve at once.

Serves 4

Redcurrant Glazed Poussins

4 x 500g (1lb) poussins, cut in half lengthwise

Redcurrant Glaze

1 tblspn butter

4 tblspn redcurrant jelly

2 tspn honey

3 tblspn lemon juice

1 Make the glaze. Heat the butter, redcurrant jelly, honey and lemon juice in a small saucepan over moderate heat, stirring frequently.

2 Brush both sides of each poussin half with the redcurrant glaze. Barbecue over moderately hot coals until cooked, basting frequently with the remaining glaze.

Serves 4

Herb Chicken Thighs

4 chicken thighs

2 tblspn chopped fresh parsley

2 tblspn chopped fresh basil

2 tblspn snipped fresh chives

3 tblspn grated Parmesan cheese

60g (2oz) mushrooms, finely chopped

2 tblspn oil

1 Ease chicken skin on each thigh gently away from flesh, taking care not to break the skin.

2 Mix the parsley, basil, chives, Parmesan and mushrooms in a small bowl. Carefully insert a quarter of the mushroom mixture between the skin and flesh on each chicken thigh, pressing the herb mixture out evenly.

3 Brush thighs generously all over with oil. Oil barbecue grill. Barbecue the chicken thighs over hot coals until cooked.

Serves 4

Barbecued Duck

2 medium ducks, halved lengthwise

Basting Sauce

125g (4oz) butter

125ml (4fl oz) lemon juice

125ml (4fl oz) red wine vinegar

2 cloves garlic, crushed

salt

freshly ground black pepper

1 Make the basting sauce. Melt the butter in a small saucepan. Stir in the lemon juice, vinegar and garlic, with salt and pepper to taste. Keep warm on the side of the barbecue grill.

2 Cook the duck halves, bone down, over moderately hot coals for 30 minutes, basting frequently with the sauce. Turn the birds over and cook, continuing to baste frequently, until the skin is crisp and golden brown.

Serves 4

Quail with Soy Honey Glaze

8 oven-ready quail

3 tblspn sesame oil

125ml (4fl oz) soy sauce

125ml (4fl oz) honey

60ml (2fl oz) lemon juice

1 Tie the legs of each quail together with string. Combine the sesame oil, soy sauce, honey and lemon juice in a small saucepan. Stir over moderate heat for 10 minutes.

2 Cook the quail over moderately hot coals until tender, turning occasionally and brushing frequently with the soy sauce mixture. Serve hot.

Serves 4

Minted Glazed Duck

30g (1oz) butter

125ml (4fl oz) redcurrant jelly

60ml (2fl oz) crème de menthe

2 onions, halved

1 medium duck, excess fat trimmed

1 bunch fresh mint

1 Melt the butter and redcurrant jelly in a small saucepan over moderate heat. Stir in the crème de menthe. Bring to the boil, lower the heat and simmer for 2 minutes. Remove from the heat.

2 Place the onion halves inside the cavity of the duck; close with skewers. Prick the duck skin all over with a fork.

3 Barbecue the duck, preferably on a rotisserie, for about 2 hours or until tender and cooked through, brushing frequently with the jelly/mint glaze. Serve, garnished with the mint.

Serves 2-3

Minted Glazed Duck

Lemon-flavoured Marinated Chicken Breasts

100ml (3½fl oz) olive oil
2 cloves garlic, finely chopped
2 tblspn chopped fresh basil
1 tblspn chopped fresh parsley
4 tblspn lemon juice
salt
freshly ground black pepper
4 chicken breast fillets

1 Combine the olive oil, garlic, basil and parsley in a small bowl. Stir in 2 tablespoons of the lemon juice and add salt and pepper to taste.

2 Arrange the chicken breasts in a single layer in a shallow dish. Pour over the olive oil mixture, cover and marinate at room temperature for 1 hour.

3 Cook the chicken breasts over hot coals until golden brown and tender, basting frequently with the marinade. Drizzle with the remaining lemon juice, cook for 1 minute more and serve.

Serves 4

Honey Ginger Grilled Chicken

1 x 1.5kg (3lb) chicken
3 tblspn honey
2 tspn ground ginger
3 tblspn Worcestershire sauce
2 tblspn soy sauce
2 cloves garlic, crushed

1 Using poultry shears, cut the chicken in half lengthwise. Remove the rib cavity. Using the palms of your hands, flatten each chicken half.

2 Heat the honey, ginger, Worcestershire sauce, soy sauce and garlic together in a small saucepan. When the mixture boils, remove the pan from the heat.

3 Brush the chicken generously with the honey ginger mixture.

4 Barbecue the chicken halves over moderately hot coals, basting frequently with the honey ginger mixture, until tender and cooked through.

Serves 4

Chicken Aioli

4 chicken quarters
125ml (4fl oz) olive oil
60ml (2fl oz) lemon juice
lemon wedges and chopped fresh parsley for garnish

Aioli

2 egg yolks
1 tblspn chopped fresh parsley
1 tblspn snipped fresh chives
2 tblspn lemon juice
4 cloves garlic, crushed
300ml (10fl oz) olive oil
salt
freshly ground black pepper

1 Arrange the chicken quarters in a single layer in a shallow bowl. Mix the oil and lemon juice together, pour the mixture over the chicken, cover and marinate for 1 hour at room temperature.

2 Make the aioli. Combine the egg yolks, fresh herbs, lemon juice and crushed garlic in a blender or food processor. Process briefly to blend. With the motor running, gradually add the oil, drop by drop, then in a steady stream, until the mixture thickens to the consistency of mayonnaise. Transfer the aioli to a bowl and add salt and pepper to taste.

3 Barbecue the chicken over hot coals until tender, basting frequently with the oil and lemon juice mixture. Garnish with the lemon wedges and chopped parsley and serve with the aioli.

Serves 4

Kitchen Tip

To save time, precook the chicken quarters in the oven or microwave.

Honey Ginger Grilled Chicken

Kashmiri Chicken with Fragrant Rice

6 chicken breast fillets

oil, see method

Marinade

155ml (5fl oz) natural low fat yogurt

1 clove garlic, finely chopped

1 tspn ground ginger

1 tblspn finely chopped fresh root ginger

1/4 tspn ground cardamom

1/4 tspn ground coriander

1 tblspn finely chopped fresh coriander

1/2 tspn salt

Fragrant Rice

3 tblspn honey

600ml (1 pt) water

375g (12oz) long-grain white rice

1/2 tspn salt

1/2 tspn ground cinnamon

30g (1oz) butter

90g (3oz) blanched almonds

90g (3oz) no-need-to-soak dried apricots, chopped

60g (2oz) currants

1 tblspn rose water

1 Make marinade by mixing all the ingredients in a small bowl.

2 Arrange chicken breasts in a single layer in a shallow dish. Pour over yogurt mixture, turn to coat well. Cover and marinate in refrigerator for 4-6 hours.

3 To make fragrant rice, dissolve honey in water in a saucepan. Add rice, salt and cinnamon, with half the butter. Bring to boil, lower heat to a bare simmer, cover pan tightly and cook for 15 minutes.

4 Melt remaining butter in a small frying pan. Sauté the almonds for 2-3 minutes. Add apricots and currants and cook for 5 minutes, stirring.

5 Tip almond mixture into the rice, cover and simmer until any remaining liquid has been absorbed and rice is tender.

6 Using tongs, transfer chicken breasts to an oiled grill over moderately hot coals. Grill, brushing occasionally with oil, until tender.

7 Stir rose water into rice. Arrange a bed of rice on each of six plates. Top with a grilled chicken breast. Serve at once.

Serves 6

Marinated Chicken Thighs

2 tblspn finely chopped root ginger

2 cloves garlic, crushed

90g (3oz) soft light brown sugar

3 tblspn Dijon mustard

60ml (2fl oz) cider vinegar

juice of 2 limes

90ml (3fl oz) olive oil

salt

freshly ground black pepper

8 chicken thighs

1 Whisk ginger, garlic, sugar, mustard, vinegar, lime juice, oil and salt and pepper to taste together.

2 Arrange thighs in a single layer in a dish, pour over ginger mixture, cover and marinate overnight in the refrigerator.

3 Grill chicken over hot coals, basting frequently with the marinade, until tender.

Serves 4

Kitchen Tip

To save time and energy, the chicken thighs may be precooked. Bake them in the marinade for 12 minutes in a 180°C (350°F/Gas 4) oven.

Basil Chicken Drumsticks

8 chicken drumsticks

30g (1oz) butter, softened

2 tblspn chopped fresh basil

2 tblspn chopped pinenuts

45g (1 1/2oz) Cheddar cheese, grated

1 tblspn finely chopped fresh parsley

1 Bring a large saucepan of water to the boil. Add chicken and allow water to return to boiling point. Lower heat and simmer for 10 minutes. Drain chicken and cool slightly.

2 Mix remaining ingredients in a small bowl; spread between the skin and flesh on each drumstick.

3 Grill over hot coals, brushing frequently with any remaining butter mixture, until golden and cooked through.

Serves 4

Poussins with Black Olive Stuffing

The best way to barbecue whole birds is on a rotisserie, but this creates problems where a stuffing is used. In the recipe below, the poussins cook to a turn over the fire while the stuffing is baked separately in the oven.

2 x 750g (1¹/₂lb) poussins
2 tblspn olive oil
1 tspn crushed peppercorns
2 tspn mixed dried herbs

Black Olive Stuffing

90g (3oz) butter
6 spring onions, finely chopped
6 rindless streaky bacon rashers, finely chopped
60g (2oz) pitted black olives, chopped
125g (4oz) dried breadcrumbs
1 tblspn chopped fresh thyme

1 Fold the neck skin over the back of each bird. Tie the wings close to the bodies, then tie the legs and tail together. Insert the rotisserie skewer lengthwise through the fleshy part of each bird so that they are well balanced and unlikely to slip when the rotisserie is turned.

2 Brush the birds with the oil. Spinkle with the peppercorns and herbs. Barbecue on the rotisserie for 1-1¹/₂ hours or until tender.

3 Meanwhile, make the stuffing. Preheat the oven to 180°C (350°F/Gas 4). Melt the butter in a saucepan over moderate heat. Add the spring onions and bacon; sauté for 3-4 minutes. Stir in the remaining ingredients, transfer to an ovenproof dish and cook for 30 minutes.

4 When ready to serve, remove the poussins from the skewer, slit the strings and cut each bird neatly in half. Serve each half with a little of the stuffing. Add a colourful vegetable garnish, if liked.

Serves 4

Basil Chicken Drumsticks

Poussins with Black Olive Stuffing

19

MEAT AND GAME

Steaks, sausages, succulent chops – meat tastes marvellous when carefully cooked over the coals.

Lamb Fillet with Mint Chutney

60ml (2fl oz) mint sauce

2 tblspn olive oil

2 cloves garlic, crushed

2 tblspn honey

750g (1¹/₂lb) lamb fillets, trimmed

watercress for garnish

Mint Chutney

185ml (6fl oz) chicken stock

60ml (2fl oz) mango chutney

2 tblspn mint jelly

1 tblspn cider vinegar

2 tspn cornflour dissolved in 1 tblspn cold water

1 Make the mint chutney. Combine the chicken stock, mango chutney, mint jelly, vinegar and cornflour mixture in a small saucepan over low heat. Bring to the boil, stirring constantly. Lower the heat and simmer until slightly thickened. Keep hot.

2 Combine the mint sauce, oil, garlic and honey in a small bowl; mix well.

3 Grill the lamb fillets over moderately hot coals until tender, turning regularly and basting with the mint sauce mixture. When the meat is cooked to taste, transfer it to a board, cut in slices and arrange around the rim of a platter. Serve the mint chutney in a bowl in the centre and garnish with the watercress.

Serves 6

Pork Kebabs with Orange Marinade

60ml (2fl oz) frozen concentrated orange juice, thawed

2 tblspn lemon juice

2 cloves garlic, crushed

60ml (2fl oz) tomato purée

1 onion, grated

1 tblspn olive oil

2 tblspn honey

500g (1lb) pork fillet, cut into 2cm (³/₄in) cubes

2 oranges

1 red pepper, cut into 2cm (³/₄in) squares

1 Soak 8 wooden skewers in warm water for 1 hour. Meanwhile, combine the citrus juices, garlic, tomato purée, grated onion, oil and honey in a shallow bowl, large enough to hold all the pork cubes in a single layer. Mix well. Stir in the pork. Marinate, covered, for 1 hour at room temperature.

2 Drain the pork, reserving the marinade. Peel and segment the oranges; cut each segment in half. Thread the pork cubes and orange pieces alternately onto the skewers.

3 Grill the pork kebabs over moderately hot coals until cooked through, basting frequently with the marinade. Serve dusted with chopped parsley, if liked.

Serves 4

Pork Kebabs with Orange Marinade, Lamb Fillet with Mint Chutney

Oriental Beef Spareribs

2kg (4lb) beef spareribs, trimmed

Marinade

125ml (4fl oz) light soy sauce

100ml (3½fl oz) lemon juice

2 cloves garlic, chopped

3 tblspn white wine vinegar

2 tblspn soft dark brown sugar

2 tblspn sesame oil

1 tblspn grated fresh root ginger

2 tspn ground coriander

½ tspn ground cumin

dash Tabasco sauce

1 Combine all the marinade ingredients in a blender or food processor; process until smooth. Spread out ribs in a single layer in a shallow dish, pour marinade over and turn to coat well. Cover and refrigerate overnight.

2 Remove ribs from marinade and grill over hot coals for about 6 minutes per side or until dark brown and crisp, turning once. Serve with a dipping sauce, if liked.

Serves 8

Lemon Lamb Chops

125ml (4fl oz) oil

2 tblspn lemon juice

1 onion, roughly chopped

2 tspn fresh oregano leaves

2 bay leaves

6 lamb loin chops

fresh herbs for garnish

1 Combine oil and lemon juice. Finely chop onion with oregano leaves by hand or in a food processor. Stir in oil mixture and add bay leaves.

2 Arrange chops in a single layer in a dish; pour over oregano marinade, cover and set aside for 30 minutes. Remove bay leaves.

3 Grill chops until tender, basting frequently with the marinade. Serve, garnished with fresh herbs.

Serves 6

Lamb Kebabs Tuscany

1.5kg (3lb) lean leg lamb, cut into 2.5cm (1in) cubes

1 green pepper, cut into 2.5cm (1in) squares

1 red pepper, cut into 2.5cm (1in) squares

2 onions, cut into eighths

Marinade

125ml (4fl oz) tomato juice

2 tblspn tomato purée

125ml (4fl oz) oil

60ml (2fl oz) red wine vinegar

3 cloves garlic, crushed

2 tspn chopped fresh oregano

½ tspn salt

½ tspn freshly ground black pepper

1 Combine marinade ingredients in a dish large enough to hold the lamb cubes in a single layer. Add the lamb, peppers and onions. Refrigerate, covered, for at least 3 hours, preferably overnight.

2 Thread the lamb, peppers and onions alternately onto oiled metal skewers. Grill over high heat until the meat is browned on the outside and pink in the centre.

Serves 8

Mustard Pork Spareribs

16 pork spareribs

1 tblspn chopped fresh rosemary

1 tblspn finely chopped garlic

salt

freshly ground black pepper

Mustard Glaze

90g (3oz) soft dark brown sugar

125ml (4fl oz) wholegrain mustard

5 tblspn cider vinegar

1 tblspn dry mustard

1 Make mustard glaze. Combine all ingredients in a saucepan. Bring to simmering, stirring constantly, cool, cover and refrigerate overnight.

2 Preheat oven to 180°C (350°F/ Gas 4). Rub spareribs with rosemary, garlic, salt and pepper. Arrange in a roasting tin; bake for 1 hour, turn once. Cool, cover and refrigerate overnight.

3 Spread meaty side of ribs with glaze. Grill skin-side down over hot coals until skin is crisp, then turn. Grill, brushing with the remaining glaze, until the ribs are crisp and glazed all over.

Serves 4

Lemon Lamb Chops

Barbecued Beef Stuffed with Herbed Vegetables

Skewered Pork

750g (1¹/₂lb) pork fillets, sliced

Marinade

1 tspn grated fresh root ginger

1 onion, finely chopped

5 tblspn soy sauce

3 tblspn soft light brown sugar

4 tblspn dry sherry

1 Make marinade. Combine the ginger, onion, soy sauce, sugar and sherry in a bowl; mix well.

2 Place pork in a single layer in a shallow dish. Pour over marinade and toss. Cover and set aside for 1 hour.

3 Thread pork onto eight oiled skewers. Grill over hot coals until tender, turning frequently and basting with the marinade. Serve at once.

Serves 4

Barbecued Beef Stuffed with Herbed Vegetables

15g (¹/₂oz) butter

1 onion, chopped

2 cloves garlic, crushed

1 red pepper, chopped

1 large courgette, finely diced

1 large carrot, finely diced

3 tblspn chopped fresh herbs

30g (1oz) fresh white breadcrumbs

30g (1oz) grated Parmesan cheese

1kg (2lb) piece of rump steak, about 5cm (2in) thick

60ml (2fl oz) olive oil

2 tblspn Dijon mustard

2 tblspn crushed black peppercorns

60ml (2fl oz) red wine

1 Make the stuffing. Heat the butter in a frying pan over moderate heat. Add the onion, garlic and pepper and cook for 1 minute. Stir in the courgette and carrot; cook for 3 minutes more. Finally stir in the herbs. Off the heat, stir in the breadcrumbs and cheese; allow the mixture to cool to room temperature.

2 Insert a knife into the side of the steak, cutting almost, but not quite through to the other side, to form a pocket. Stuff the vegetable mixture firmly into the pocket; close the opening with string.

3 Mix the oil, mustard, pepper and wine in a bowl. Grill the steak over moderately hot coals until cooked as desired, basting frequently with the oil mixture and turning every 15 minutes.

Serves 6

Pork Brochettes with Spicy Yogurt Marinade

375ml (12fl oz) natural low fat yogurt

1 onion, finely chopped

2 cloves garlic, crushed

2 tspn sambal oelek or 1 tblspn sweet chilli sauce

1 tblspn freshly squeezed lime juice

1 tspn ground cumin

1 tblspn chopped fresh coriander

500g (1lb) pork fillet, trimmed and cut into 2cm (³/₄in) cubes

90g (3oz) dried apricots

1 Combine yogurt, onion, garlic, sambal oelek, lime juice, cumin and coriander in a bowl. Mix well.

2 Arrange the pork cubes in a single layer in a large shallow dish. Add the apricots. Pour the yogurt mixture into the dish, mix well, cover and refrigerate for 6 hours or overnight.

3 Drain the pork and apricots, reserving the marinade. Thread the pork cubes and apricots alternately onto oiled metal or soaked wooden skewers. Grill over moderately hot coals, turning occasionally and basting with marinade, until pork is cooked and apricots are tender.

Serves 4

Tandoori Beef Ribs

8 beef spareribs, trimmed

2 tblspn oil

Marinade

250ml (8fl oz) natural low fat yogurt

1¹/₂ tspn grated fresh root ginger

2 cloves garlic, crushed

1 tblspn sweet chilli sauce

1 tspn ground cumin

1 tspn ground cardamom

1 tblspn finely chopped fresh coriander

few drops of red food colouring

1 tblspn tamarind paste

125ml (4fl oz) water

1 Make the marinade. Combine the yogurt, ginger, garlic, chilli sauce, cumin, cardamom, coriander and food colouring in a bowl. Mix well. Blend the tamarind paste with water; fold into the yogurt mixture.

2 Rub the marinade into the spareribs. Arrange in a shallow dish. Set aside, covered, for at least 3 hours, preferably overnight.

3 Remove the ribs from the marinade and grill over hot coals until dark brown and crisp, turning once and basting with the remaining marinade.

Serves 4

Barbecued Steak Thai-style

3 cloves garlic, chopped

1 chilli, seeded and roughly chopped

1 large onion, quartered

1 bunch fresh coriander, stripped from stems

5 tblspn freshly squeezed lime juice

60ml (2fl oz) Thai fish sauce

2 tblspn soft light brown sugar

salt

6 large or 12 small minute steaks

1 Process garlic, chilli and onion briefly in a food processor. Add coriander leaves (with a few tender stems, if liked) and process until finely chopped. Add lime juice, fish sauce and sugar, with salt to taste. Process for 30 seconds. Transfer to a small saucepan; heat gently.

2 Brush both sides of steaks with the spicy mixture. Grill over hot coals for 1-2 minutes, constantly brushing with more of the spicy mixture. Spoon any remaining mixture over steaks when serving.

Serves 6

Lamb Kebabs with Peanut Sauce

750g (1¹/₂lb) lean minced lamb

3 tblspn chopped fresh parsley

1 tspn dried oregano

2 tspn ground cumin

2 tblspn tomato purée

2 onions, very finely chopped

90g (3oz) dried breadcrumbs

2 egg whites

oil for greasing grill

Sauce

1 tblspn peanut oil

2 cloves garlic, crushed

1 onion, finely chopped

125g (4oz) crunchy peanut butter

1 tspn tomato purée

2 tblspn sweet fruit chutney

2 tblspn sherry

1 tblspn lemon juice

5 tblspn coconut cream

2 tspn ground coriander

1 tspn sambal oelek or Tabasco sauce to taste

1 Soak 8 wooden skewers in warm water for 1 hour. Combine lamb, parsley, oregano, cumin, tomato purée, onions, breadcrumbs and egg whites. Mix well. Form into eight sausage shapes and thread onto drained skewers.

2 Make sauce. Heat oil in a saucepan. Add garlic and onion and fry for 2 minutes. Stir in peanut butter, tomato purée, chutney, sherry, lemon juice, coconut cream, coriander and sambal oelek and stir cooking over low heat until mixture thickens slightly. Set aside keep hot.

3 Cook kebabs on an oiled grill over hot coals, turning once, until golden brown and cooked through. Serve with sauce.

Serves 4

Pork Brochettes with Spicy Yogurt Marinade, Lamb Kebabs with Peanut Sauce

Pepper Beef Fillet with Watercress Sauce

Pepper Beef Fillet with Watercress Sauce

60g (2oz) butter, softened
2 cloves garlic, crushed
3 tblspn crushed black peppercorns
750g (1¹/₂lb) fillet of beef, trimmed
125g (4oz) watercress
1 egg yolk
2 tspn Dijon mustard
¹/₄ tspn salt
¹/₄ tspn grated nutmeg
185ml (6fl oz) light olive oil
1 tblspn freshly squeezed lime juice
60ml (2fl oz) double cream

1 Preheat oven to 180°C (350°F/ Gas 4). Beat butter and garlic together in a small bowl. Spread out crushed peppercorns on a piece of foil. Coat meat with garlic butter and roll in peppercorns until coated.

2 Cook beef fillet on a rotisserie, or on an oiled grill over hot coals, turning frequently, until done to your personal taste. Transfer to a platter, cover with a tent of foil and allow to stand for 10 minutes.

3 Set aside about a third of the watercress sprigs for garnish. Strip the remaining leaves from the stems as the basis for the sauce.

4 Combine the egg yolk, mustard, salt and nutmeg in a blender or food processor. Process until smooth. With the motor running, add the oil through the feeder tube, at first drop by drop, then in a steady stream. When the sauce starts to thicken, add the watercress leaves; process until finely chopped. Transfer the sauce to a bowl, beat in the lime juice, then add the cream and mix well.

5 Slice the beef. Fan out the slices on a platter garnished with the reserved watercress. Spoon a little of the watercress sauce down the centre of the meat slices; serve the remaining sauce separately.

Serves 4

Tandoori Lamb Cutlets

8 lamb cutlets, trimmed
Marinade
125ml (4fl oz) natural low fat yogurt
1 tspn grated fresh root ginger
1 clove garlic, crushed
1 tblspn freshly squeezed lime juice
1 tspn ground cumin
¹/₄ tspn ground cardamom
¹/₄ tspn chilli powder
¹/₄ tspn garam masala
few drops red food colouring

1 Arrange lamb cutlets in a single layer in a large shallow dish. Make marinade. Combine yogurt, ginger, garlic, lime juice, cumin, cardamom, chilli powder and garam masala with enough colouring to give mixture a pink tint. Pour over cutlets, toss to coat, cover and marinate for 30 minutes at room temperature.

2 Grill cutlets over hot coals until tender, basting with marinade.

Serves 4

Pork Kebabs with Peppers and Onions

750g (1¹/₂lb) pork fillet, trimmed, cut into cubes
60ml (2fl oz) olive oil
1 tblspn red wine vinegar
2-3 tblspn snipped chives
salt
freshly ground black pepper
2 red peppers, cut into squares
2 yellow peppers, cut into squares
2 onions, quartered

1 Spread out the pork cubes in a single layer in a shallow dish. Whisk the oil, vinegar and chives in a bowl, add salt and pepper to taste and pour over the meat. Mix well. Cover and marinate for 1 hour at room temperature.

2 Drain the meat, discarding the marinade. Thread the pork cubes, peppers and onion quarters alternately onto oiled metal skewers. Grill over hot coals until tender, turning once.

Serves 6

Sticky Ribs

30g (1oz) butter

2 cloves garlic, crushed

250ml (8fl oz) tomato ketchup

4 tblspn Worcestershire sauce

5 tblspn malt vinegar

5 tblspn soft light brown sugar

1 tspn sweet chilli sauce

1/4 tspn crushed black peppercorns

2kg (4lb) pork spareribs, trimmed

1 Melt the butter in a frying pan over gentle heat. Add the garlic and cook for 1 minute. Stir in the tomato ketchup, Worcestershire sauce, vinegar, sugar, chilli sauce and pepper. Mix well; simmer, uncovered, for 10 minutes.

2 Barbecue ribs over moderately hot coals until tender, brushing liberally at frequent intervals with the tomato ketchup mixture.

Serves 6-8

Pork Chops with Orange Glaze

4 large pork chops, about 3cm (1¹/₄in) thick

2 tblspn soy sauce

2 tblspn honey

2 cloves garlic, crushed

1 tblspn freshly grated root ginger

1 tblspn finely grated orange rind

185ml (6fl oz) frozen concentrated orange juice, thawed

1 tblspn orange marmalade

2 tblspn lemon juice

15g (¹/₂oz) butter

1 Using a very sharp knife, score pork chops 3mm (¹/₈in) deep, in a criss-cross pattern. Arrange in a single layer in a shallow dish.

2 Combine soy sauce, honey, garlic, ginger, rind, orange juice, marmalade and lemon juice in a bowl; mix well. Pour mixture over chops, toss to coat, cover and refrigerate for 1 hour.

3 Drain chops, reserving the marinade in a small saucepan. Grill chops over moderately hot coals until tender, basting frequently with marinade. Place pan containing remaining marinade over high heat, stirring until reduced by about one third. Serve with chops.

Serves 4

Bacon and Sausage Kebabs

8 chipolata sausages or frankfurters

8 rindless streaky bacon rashers

1 red pepper, cut into eight 2.5cm (1in) squares

12 button mushrooms

8 cherry tomatoes, halved

8 shallots, peeled

60g (2oz) butter, softened

1 tblspn Dijon mustard

1 tspn lemon juice

1 Twist each chipolata sausage in half and cut through to make 16 small sausages. Spear the end of a bacon rasher with a long oiled skewer. Add a mini sausage and weave the bacon around; pierce the bacon again. Add a red pepper square, a mushroom, a tomato, a shallot and another sausage in the same way, then introduce another bacon rasher and repeat the sequence, ending with an extra mushroom. Make three more kebabs in the same way.

2 Melt the butter, mustard and lemon juice in a small saucepan, stirring constantly. Brush the mixture over the kebabs.

3 Grill over hot coals, turning occasionally, until the bacon is crisp and the sausages are cooked through. Serve at once.

Serves 4

Sticky Ribs, Pork Chops with Orange Glaze

Hamburgers

500g (1lb) minced lean steak

salt

freshly ground black pepper

2 tblspn finely chopped onion

Mix all ingredients together. Divide mixture into 4 portions and shape into plump patties. Grill burgers over hot coals for about 4 minutes on each side or until done to your taste. Serve in burger baps, with salad and a selection of relishes.

Serves 4-6

Variations
The best burgers are pure meat, but the mixture may be stretched with a little finely grated carrot, breadcrumbs or wheatgerm. Add 1 teaspoon Worcestershire or soy sauce for extra flavour, if liked. For a surprise centre, mould each patty around 1 teaspoon grated Cheddar cheese, crumbled blue cheese or sweet pickle.

Curried Pitta Patties

500g (1lb) minced lean steak

2 tblspn finely chopped onion

1 clove garlic, crushed

1 tblspn curry paste

1/4 tspn ground ginger

1/4 tspn ground cumin

4 pitta breads

shredded lettuce and natural low fat yogurt to serve

1 Mix minced steak, onion, garlic, curry paste, ginger and cumin together in a bowl. Divide mixture into four portions and shape into oval patties to fit the pitta pockets.

2 Grill patties over hot coals for about 4 minutes on each side or until done to your taste.

3 Meanwhile, warm pitta breads at side of barbecue grill. Slit the breads, open out pockets and add a patty to each. Top with shredded lettuce and serve with yogurt.

Serves 4

Zesty Rabbit Burgers

500g (1lb) rabbit meat, cut into chunks

1 egg yolk, beaten

2 tblspn fresh white breadcrumbs

3 tblspn tomato purée

salt

freshly ground black pepper

1 Grind rabbit finely in a food processor. Place in a bowl, with egg, breadcrumbs and tomato purée and salt and pepper to taste. Mix well. Shape into four patties. Chill for 30 minutes.

2 Fix a piece of oiled foil to the barbecue grill, taking care to leave some spaces so that the air supply to the fire is not cut off.

3 Barbecue burgers on foil over moderately hot coals until well cooked. Serve in buns.

Serves 4

Marinated Beef Strips

1kg (2lb) rump steak, cut crosswise into long flat strips

1 large onion, sliced in rings

5 tblspn olive oil

250ml (8fl oz) red wine

4 cloves garlic, chopped

1 tblspn black peppercorns

30g (1oz) fresh parsley, leaves stripped from stems

1 tblspn fresh thyme leaves

1 cucumber, shaved into thin slices with a vegetable peeler

1 Arrange steak and onion in a single layer in a dish. Combine oil, wine, garlic, peppercorns, parsley and thyme and pour over steak and mix lightly. Cover and refrigerate for 4 hours or preferably overnight.

2 Drain meat. Weave strips onto oiled metal or soaked wooden skewers; grill over hot coals until tender. Serve on a bed of shaved cucumber.

Serves 8

Marinated Beef Strips

SALADS AND SIDE DISHES

Add bright colours and crisp fresh flavours to your barbecue feasts with this selection of superb salads, sauces and vegetable dishes

Watercress and Red Cabbage Salad

Serve this colourful salad with pork kebabs or sausages.

250g (8oz) watercress

185g (6oz) red cabbage, finely shredded

6 hard-boiled eggs, finely chopped

Dressing

1¹/₂ tblspn red wine vinegar

1 tspn Dijon mustard

5 tblspn salad oil

3 tblspn olive oil

2 tblspn mayonnaise

salt

freshly ground black pepper

1 Make the dressing. Combine the vinegar, mustard, oils and mayonnaise in a screwtop jar. Close the lid tightly; shake well. Add salt and pepper to taste.

2 Break the watercress into sprigs, removing any tough stalks. Toss with the red cabbage in a large bowl.

3 Pour half the dressing over the salad; toss to coat well. Add the egg, mix lightly and serve at once. Offer the remaining dressing separately.

Serves 8

Grapefruit and Avocado Salad with Bacon

2 grapefruit

2 avocados, halved, stoned, peeled and thinly sliced lengthwise

juice of ¹/₂ lemon

salt

1 tblspn olive oil

250g (8oz) rindless streaky bacon rashers, cut into 5mm (¹/₄in) strips

¹/₂ tspn sugar

freshly ground black pepper

1 Peel and segment the grapefruit, taking care to remove the pith. Cut about a quarter of the grapefruit peel into julienne strips; blanch in a small saucepan of boiling water for 1 minute, then drain and pat dry.

2 Lightly toss the avocado slices in the lemon juice in a bowl. Drain, reserving the lemon juice. Sprinkle the avocado slices lightly with salt. Arrange avocado and grapefruit alternately on a large platter.

3 Heat the oil in a frying pan, add the bacon and fry until crisp. Stir in the sugar and reserved lemon juice, with pepper to taste. Heat through.

4 Pour the bacon mixture over the avocado and grapefruit. Garnish with the julienned grapefruit peel. Serve at once.

Serves 4

Basil, Orange and Peach Salad

Basil, Orange and Peach Salad

1 bunch fresh basil

6 oranges, peeled and segmented

3 peaches, skinned and sliced

1 red onion, sliced

2 tblspn red wine vinegar

1 garlic clove, crushed

2 tblspn unsweetened apple juice

2 tblspn salad oil

1 Wash and dry the basil leaves. Arrange on a salad platter.

2 In a bowl, combine the orange segments, peach slices and onion.

3 Mix the vinegar, garlic, apple juice and oil in a screwtop jar. Close the lid tightly and shake well. Pour the dressing over the orange mixture; toss well.

4 Arrange the dressed oranges, peaches and onion on the basil. Serve at once.

Serves 6

Mustard Potatoes

1kg (2lb) new potatoes

60ml (2fl oz) soured cream

60ml (2fl oz) mayonnaise

2 tblspn grainy mustard

2 tblspn French dressing

1 Cook the potatoes in a large saucepan of boiling water until just tender. Rub off the skins and set the potatoes aside to cool.

2 Mix the soured cream, mayonnaise, mustard and French dressing in a small bowl. Spoon the mixture over the potatoes. Serve at room temperature.

Serves 4

Variation
Use 1 tspn garam masala instead of the mustard for a mild curry flavour.

Cauliflower, Tomato and Courgette Salad

1 cauliflower, divided into florets

4 courgettes, cut into 2.5cm (1in) slices

1 soft round lettuce, separated into leaves

1 mignonette lettuce, separated into leaves

4 ripe tomatoes, cut into wedges

roughly chopped fresh parsley for garnish

Dressing

2 cloves garlic, roughly chopped

2 tblspn roughly chopped parsley stalks

90g (3oz) walnut halves

2 tblspn cold water

100ml (3¹/2fl oz) walnut oil

100ml (3¹/2fl oz) salad oil

2 tspn lemon juice

salt

freshly ground black pepper

1 Make the dressing. Finely chop the garlic, parsley and walnuts in a food processor. Add the water and mix to a purée. With the motor running, gradually add the oils through the feeder tube in a steady steam, then add the lemon juice. Add salt and pepper to taste.

2 Steam the cauliflower for 2 minutes, then add the courgettes and steam for 2 minutes or until both vegetables are crisp-cooked. Refresh under cold running water; drain well.

3 Mix the salad leaves together in a large salad bowl. Toss in the cauliflower, courgettes and tomato wedges. Pour half the dressing over the salad and toss well to coat. Sprinkle with the parsley. Serve at once, offering the remaining dressing separately.

Serves 6

Mangetout Salad

375g (12oz) French beans, topped and tailed

375g (12oz) mangetout, trimmed

Dressing

1¹/2 tblspn salad oil

1¹/2 tblspn sesame seeds

1¹/2 tblspn white wine vinegar

1 tspn sugar

1 tspn soy sauce

1 Make the dressing. Heat the oil in a frying pan over moderate heat. Add sesame seeds and cook until light brown. Off the heat, stir in vinegar, sugar and soy sauce.

2 Blanch beans and mangetout in boiling water. Drain vegetables and refresh under cold water. Drain again. Place vegetables into a salad bowl, add the dressing and toss well. Serve at once.

Serves 6

Spinach Salad with Roquefort Dressing

1 tblspn olive oil

3 rindless streaky bacon rashers, finely chopped

90g (3oz) slivered almonds

375g (12oz) young spinach, roughly chopped

30g (1oz) Roquefort cheese, crumbled

1 tblspn mayonnaise

1 tblspn soured cream

60ml (2fl oz) single cream

1 Heat the oil in a large frying pan over moderate heat. Add the bacon and cook until crisp. Add the almonds to the pan and cook for about 3 minutes, or until golden.

2 Arrange spinach on a serving platter, add bacon and almonds and toss lightly.

3 In a small bowl, combine cheese, mayonnaise, soured cream and cream. Mix well. Pour dressing over salad just before serving.

Serves 4

Spinach Salad with Roquefort Dressing

Warm Lettuce Salad with Mushrooms

60ml (2fl oz) olive oil

2 cloves garlic, crushed

125g (4oz) large mushrooms, sliced

1 large Iceberg lettuce, shredded

1 tblspn lemon juice

90g (3oz) drained canned mandarin
orange segments

1 Heat the oil in a large frying pan over moderate heat. Stir in the garlic and mushrooms and cook for 2 minutes.

2 Stir in the shredded lettuce, lemon juice, mandarins and orange segments. Toss well and serve at once.

Serves 4

Broccoli Salad with Hazelnuts

250g (8oz) broccoli florets

45g (1¹/₂oz) hazelnuts, sliced

Dressing

60ml (2fl oz) natural low fat yogurt

1 tblspn lemon juice

1 small clove garlic, crushed

2 tblspn finely chopped onion

1 tblspn tomato ketchup

dash Tabasco sauce

1 Steam the broccoli for about 3 minutes or until crisp-cooked. Refresh under cold running water; drain well and cool.

2 Whisk the dressing ingredients together in a small bowl. Refrigerate, covered, for at least 1 hour.

3 Preheat oven to 180°C (350°F/ Gas 4). Spread out the hazelnuts on a baking sheet; toast until pale brown; cool.

4 Place the broccoli in a salad bowl, add the chilled dressing and toss well. Sprinkle with the toasted hazelnuts. Serve at once.

Serves 4

Bean and Pepper Medley

Coriander, Mushroom and Tomato Salad

2 bunches fresh coriander, roughly chopped

375g (12oz) button mushrooms, sliced

500g (1lb) cherry tomatoes, halved

Dressing

1 tblspn Dijon mustard

1¹/₂ tblspn red wine vinegar

90ml (3fl oz) olive oil

salt

freshly ground black pepper

1 Combine coriander, mushrooms and tomatoes in a salad bowl.

2 Make the dressing. Combine the mustard and vinegar in a small bowl. Gradually whisk in the oil; add salt and pepper to taste.

3 Pour the dressing over the salad; toss to coat. Serve at once.

Serves 6

Bean and Pepper Medley

250g (8oz) green beans, topped, tailed and cut into 2cm (³/₄in) lengths

250g (8oz) drained canned red kidney beans, rinsed

¹/₂ red pepper, cut into very thin strips

thinly pared rind and juice of 1 orange

2 tblspn red wine vinegar

3 tblspn olive oil

¹/₄ tspn crushed black peppercorns

2 tspn finely chopped fresh tarragon

1 Cook green beans in a large saucepan of boiling water for about 3 minutes or until crisp-tender; drain, refresh under cold running water; drain again.

2 Tip beans into a salad bowl. Add kidney beans, red pepper and orange rind.

3 Whisk orange juice, vinegar, oil, crushed peppercorns and tarragon in a small bowl, pour over the salad and toss well.

Serves 4

Green Salad with Pecans

125g (4oz) mangetout, trimmed

1 Iceberg lettuce, roughly shredded

4 radishes, sliced

1 stick celery, sliced

45g (1¹/₂oz) pecan nuts

60ml (2fl oz) olive oil

1 tblspn red wine vinegar

1 tblspn rice wine vinegar or sherry vinegar

pinch dried oregano

pinch dried basil

1 Preheat oven to 180°C (350°F/ Gas 4). Boil, steam or microwave the mangetout for 1 minute; drain. Refresh under cold running water; drain again.

2 Combine the lettuce, radishes, mangetout and celery in a salad bowl. Spread out the pecans on a baking sheet; toast in the oven for 5 minutes. When cool, add to the salad bowl.

3 Combine the oil, vinegars and herbs in a screwtop jar. Close the lid tightly and shake well. Pour the dressing over the salad; toss well.

Serves 4

Celery Salad

6 sticks celery, diagonally sliced

60g (2oz) feta cheese, crumbled

1 hard-boiled egg, sliced

30g (1oz) black olives

5 tblspn olive oil

3 tblspn red wine vinegar

1 Arrange the celery slices, cheese, egg slices and olives on a salad platter.

2 Whisk the oil and vinegar together in a small bowl. Drizzle a little of the dressing over the salad and serve the rest separately.

Serves 4

Avocado Salad

2 avocados, halved, stoned and peeled

1 tomato

1 red pepper

1 cucumber

8 black olives

Dressing

1 tblspn honey

3 tblspn cider vinegar

5 tblspn olive oil

salt

freshly ground black pepper

1 Cut avocados into 2cm (³/₄in) cubes. Cut tomato, red pepper and cucumber into cubes of a similar size. Place vegetables and olives in a salad bowl.

2 Make dressing by whisking the honey, vinegar, oil and salt and pepper to taste together. Drizzle a little dressing over salad and serve the rest separately.

Serves 4

Broad Bean and Tomato Salad

Illustrated on page 9

500g (1lb) shelled broad beans

30g (1oz) pitted black olives, sliced

500g (1lb) tomatoes, cut in thin wedges

2 tblspn chopped fresh parsley

60ml (2fl oz) olive oil

2 cloves garlic, crushed

¹/₂ tspn freshly ground black pepper

2 tblspn red wine vinegar

1 Blanch broad beans in boiling water, drain and refresh under cold running water. Drain again. Place broad beans, olives, tomatoes and parsley in a salad bowl.

2 Whisk olive oil, garlic, pepper and vinegar in a small bowl. Pour over salad and toss well.

Serves 4

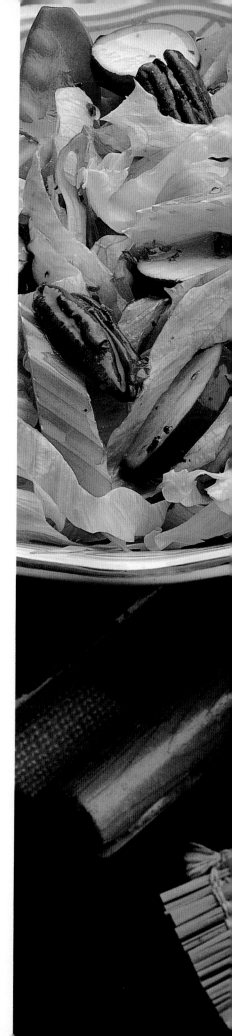

Green Salad with Pecans, Avocado Salad

Honey Baked Parsnips and Carrots

60g (2oz) butter

2 cloves garlic, crushed

2 tblspn lemon juice

2 tblspn honey

4 carrots, halved lengthwise

4 tender young parsnips, halved lengthwise

1 Preheat oven to 180°C (350°F/ Gas 4). Melt the butter in a medium saucepan over gentle heat. Add the garlic and cook for 1 minute. Stir in the lemon juice and honey; mix well.

2 Arrange the vegetables in a baking dish. Brush with the honey mixture and bake for 25 minutes, basting frequently.

Serves 4

Grated Courgette Sauté

45g (1¹/₂oz) butter

1 small onion, very finely chopped

¹/₄ tspn grated nutmeg

3 large courgettes

1 Melt the butter in a medium frying pan over moderate heat. Add the onion and cook for 3-4 minutes until softened but not browned. Stir in the nutmeg.

2 Trim the courgettes, then grate them coarsely. Add the grated courgettes to the pan; toss in the hot onion butter until tender. Serve immediately.

Serves 4

Fresh Tomato Sauce

2 tblspn olive oil

1 large onion, chopped

1 clove garlic, crushed

1 x 397g (13oz) can chopped tomatoes

¹/₄ tspn sugar

125ml (4fl oz) dry white wine

2 tblspn chopped fresh basil

freshly ground black pepper

Heat the oil in a saucepan, add the onion and garlic and cook for 4-5 minutes, until softened. Stir in the tomatoes, sugar and wine; simmer for 5 minutes. Add half the basil; simmer for 1 hour or until the sauce is thick and flavoursome. Just before serving, stir in the remaining basil, with pepper to taste. Serve with seafood, chicken, steaks or sausages.

Makes about 600ml (1pt)

Barbecue Sauce

60g (2oz) butter

¹/₂ mild onion, chopped

60ml (2fl oz) red wine vinegar

125ml (4fl oz) water

2 tblspn soft light brown sugar

2 tspn Dijon mustard

¹/₂ tspn salt

1 tspn freshly ground black pepper

¹/₄ tspn paprika

1 thick slice lemon

250ml (8fl oz) tomato ketchup

1 tblspn Worcestershire sauce

1 tspn soy sauce

Melt the butter in a saucepan. Add the onion and cook for 2-3 minutes. Stir in the vinegar, water, sugar, mustard, salt, pepper and paprika. Add the lemon slice. Simmer for 30 minutes, stirring occasionally. Remove the lemon; stir in the remaining ingredients and cook for 15 minutes more. Use as a basting sauce or an accompaniment.

Makes about 500ml (16fl oz)

Potatoes with Red Peppers

3 large potatoes, cut into 5mm (¼in) slices

2 onions, chopped

2 red peppers, cut into thin strips

2 rindless streaky bacon rashers, cut into thin strips

1 tblspn chopped fresh sage

½ tspn crushed black peppercorns

60ml (2fl oz) olive oil

sage sprig for garnish

1 Preheat oven to 180°C (350°F/ Gas 4). Mix potatoes, onions, pepper strips and bacon in a large baking dish.

2 Combine the sage, peppercorns and olive oil in a bowl; mix lightly. Pour the mixture over the vegetables. Bake for 40 minutes, turning vegetables occasionally. Garnish with the fresh sage.

Serves 6

Fresh Pea Casserole with Prosciutto

3 tblspn olive oil

30g (1oz) butter

1 onion, chopped

6 slices of prosciutto, cut into strips

500g (1lb) shelled peas

250ml (8fl oz) water

1 tblspn chopped fresh mint

mint sprig for garnish

1 Heat the oil with the butter in a large frying pan. Add the onion and prosciutto and cook for 3 minutes over moderate heat.

2 Add peas and measured water. Bring to boil, then lower heat. Simmer peas for about 20 minutes or until tender.

3 Strain peas, transfer to a serving dish. Toss with chopped mint. Serve at once, garnished with mint sprig.

Serves 4

Potatoes with Red Peppers, Fresh Pea Casserole with Prosciutto

Peppered Garlic Leeks

Peppered Garlic Leeks

3 large leeks, white parts only

½ tspn crushed black peppercorns

60ml (2fl oz) olive oil

2 small cloves garlic, crushed

2 tblspn lime juice

1 Cut the leeks into long thin strips. Rinse, drain and pat dry with paper towels. Toss leeks with peppercorns.

2 Heat oil in a frying pan over moderate heat. Add garlic, lower heat and cook for 2 minutes, see Kitchen Tip.

3 Stir in leeks. Stir fry for 2 minutes, constantly lifting the leeks with 2 spatulas and allowing them to drop back into the pan. Transfer leeks to a warm bowl, toss with the lime juice and serve at once.

Serves 4

Kitchen Tip
When frying a small amount of garlic like this, it is very easy to burn it, with disastrous consequences in terms of flavour. Keep the heat low, stir the garlic frequently, and remove the pan from the heat if the garlic starts to darken.

Caramelised Onions

60g (2oz) butter

500g (1lb) pickling onions, peeled

salt

freshly ground black pepper

2 tspn sugar

5 tblspn red wine

1 Preheat oven to 180°C (350°F/ Gas 4). Melt the butter in a frying pan large enough to hold the onions comfortably in a single layer. Add the onions. Season with a little salt and pepper.

2 Brown the onions all over, shaking the pan from time to time. Add the sugar and continue to cook until it caramelises.

3 Transfer the onions to a small roasting tin. Stir in the wine. Roast for 30 minutes or until tender. Serve hot.

Serves 4

Bacon Roast Potatoes, Jacket Potatoes with Feta Filling

Bacon Roast Potatoes

4 large potatoes, quartered

60ml (2fl oz) oil

1 tblspn hazelnut oil

2 tspn salt

6 rindless streaky bacon rashers, finely chopped

1/4 tspn white pepper

1/4 tspn grated nutmeg

1 Preheat oven to 180°C (350°F/ Gas 4). Bring a large saucepan of water to the boil. Add potatoes and cook for 5 minutes; drain. Pat dry with paper towels.

2 Transfer potatoes to a roasting tin. Drizzle the oils over top and toss to coat. Sprinkle with the salt.

3 Roast potatoes for 30 minutes, turning occasionally. Sprinkle bacon, pepper and nutmeg over potatoes; cook for 10 minutes more or until bacon is crisp.

Serves 4-6

Jacket Potatoes with Feta Filling

4 large baking potatoes

30g (1oz) butter

60g (2oz) feta cheese, cubed

30g (1oz) grated Parmesan cheese

2 spring onions, finely chopped

2 tblspn chopped hazelnuts

1 Preheat oven to 200°C (400°F/ Gas 6). Bake potatoes directly on an oven shelf for 1 hour or until soft. Cut off tops and carefully scoop pulp into a bowl, keeping the shells intact.

2 Mash potato pulp with butter. Stir in feta cubes, Parmesan and spring onions. Pile mixture back into potato shells, top with chopped hazelnuts and return the potatoes to the oven for 15 minutes to heat through. Serve at once.

Serves 4

DRINKS AND DESSERTS

When the flames flicker, what better way to cool off than with a pitcher of punch or a soothing sorbet? This chapter is packed with refreshing suggestions, plus warming drinks and desserts for those occasions when the weather is less than welcoming.

White Sangria

1 bottle Chardonnay, chilled

1 small bottle bitter lemon, chilled

2 tblspn Cointreau

1 large ripe peach, sliced

1 large nectarine, sliced

1 large orange, sliced

125g (4oz) seedless green grapes

Combine all the ingredients in a large jug. Stir well, cover and refrigerate for 2 hours.

Serves 6-8

Bloody Mary Punch

2 litres (3¹/₂pt) tomato juice

125ml (4fl oz) lemon juice

250ml (8fl oz) vodka

2 tspn Worcestershire sauce

salt

freshly ground black pepper

1 litre (1³/4pt) soda water, chilled

thin lemon slices for garnish

1 Combine the tomato juice, lemon juice, vodka and Worcestershire sauce in a large jug. Add salt and freshly ground black pepper to taste. Chill for several hours.

2 When ready to serve, stir in the chilled soda water. Garnish with lemon slices.

Serves 12

Peach Punch

1 x 440g (14oz) can peaches, drained and chopped

60ml (2fl oz) peach brandy

1 bottle chilled still dry white wine

1 bottle sparkling white wine

1 Combine the peaches, peach brandy and dry white wine in a punch bowl or large jug. Cover and chill for several hours.

2 Stir in the sparkling wine just before serving.

Serves 10

Lime and Lemonade

185g (6oz) sugar

250ml (8fl oz) water

60ml (2fl oz) freshly squeezed lime juice

185ml (6fl oz) lemon juice

750ml (1¹/4pt) soda water, chilled

lemon slices for garnish

1 Combine the sugar and water in a saucepan. Stir over low heat until the sugar has dissolved. Boil, without stirring, for 2 minutes; cool.

2 Combine the sugar syrup, lime juice and lemon juice in a punch bowl or large jug. Add the soda water just before serving. Garnish with lemon slices.

Serves 6

Lime and Lemonade

Tequila Mary

Jamaican Banana Punch

90g (3oz) icing sugar

1 tspn grated nutmeg

1 tspn ground cinnamon

¹/₂ tspn ground cloves

185ml (6fl oz) soda water

2 litres (3¹/₂pt) dark rum

750ml (1¹/₄pt) banana liqueur

1 litre (1³/₄pt) pineapple juice

1 litre (1³/₄pt) orange juice

1 litre (1³/₄pt) lemon juice

4 bananas

1 Combine the icing sugar, nutmeg, cinnamon and cloves in a jug. Add the soda water and stir until the sugar has dissolved.

2 Place a large block of ice in a punch bowl. Add the rum and banana liqueur. Stir in the pineapple, orange and lemon juices, with the soda water mixture. Stir gently to combine. Slice the bananas into the punch just before serving.

Serves 24

Riesling Strawberry Punch

10 strawberries

1¹/₂ tblspn sugar

2 bottles Riesling

185ml (6fl oz) kirsch

750ml (1¹/₄pt) soda water, chilled

1 Place the strawberries in a bowl with the sugar. Slightly bruise the berries. Cover the bowl and set aside to macerate for at least 1 hour.

2 Pour the wine and kirsch into a punch bowl. Cover and refrigerate. When ready to serve, add the strawberries, with their juices, and chilled soda water to the bowl. Serve 1 strawberry in each cup or glass.

Serves 10

Tequila Mary

500ml (16fl oz) tomato juice

5 tblspn lemon juice

2 spring onions, finely chopped

1 tspn sugar

few drops Tabasco sauce

125ml (4fl oz) Tequila

1 Combine the tomato juice, lemon juice, spring onions, sugar and Tabasco in a blender or food processor; process until smooth.

2 Divide the Tequila between four serving glasses. Add the tomato mixture, still well and serve, garnished with parsley if liked.

Serves 4

Hot Armagnac

750ml (1¹/₄pt) dry red wine

1 x 5cm (2in) cinnamon stick

pinch grated nutmeg

6 cloves

3 tblspn honey

5 tblspn lemon juice

4 tblspn Armagnac

1 Combine red wine, cinnamon, nutmeg, cloves, honey and lemon juice in a saucepan. Bring to just below boiling point over gentle heat.

2 Warm four mugs by filling them with boiling water, tipping water away and drying thoroughly. Strain hot wine mixture into each mug; stir 1 tablespoon of Armagnac into each. Stir gently and serve.

Serves 4

Strawberry Mousse

60ml (2fl oz) orange juice

1 tblspn powdered gelatine

500g (1lb) strawberries, puréed

1 tblspn cherry brandy

3 egg whites

3 tblspn caster sugar

1 Combine the orange juice and gelatine in a cup. Add the mixture to strawberry purée and mix to combine. Pour into a saucepan.

2 Place the pan over low heat, stirring constantly until the gelatine has dissolved. Pour the mixture into a bowl; stir in the cherry brandy. Cool, cover bowl and refrigerate until on the point of setting.

3 Beat eggs in a grease-free bowl until soft peaks form. Gradually add sugar, beating until stiff. Fold into strawberry mixture. Transfer mixture to a serving bowl or soufflé dish; chill for 4 hours or until the mousse sets.

Serves 6

Barbecued Bananas with Rum

6 large slightly green bananas

melted butter, see method

1 tblspn freshly squeezed lime juice

2 tblspn soft light brown sugar

1 tblspn rum

1 Cut the unpeeled bananas in half lengthwise. Brush the cut sides with melted butter, then sear, cut side down, on an oiled grill over hot coals.

2 Turn the bananas over and move them a cooler part of the grill. Sprinkle with lime juice, sugar and rum and cook until the skins have blackened and the flesh is soft. Serve in the skins.

Serves 6

Orange Segments in Red Wine Syrup

6 oranges, peeled and segmented

4 tblspn honey

4 tblspn soft light brown sugar

4 tblspn lemon juice

250ml (8fl oz) red wine

1 Arrange the orange segments in four serving glasses.

2 Heat the honey, sugar, lemon juice and red wine in a saucepan over high heat, stirring constantly. Bring to the boil, lower the heat and simmer until the syrup has reduced by half and has thickened slightly.

3 Allow the syrup to cool slightly before pouring it over the orange segments. If using glass dishes, pour the syrup over a spoon. Serve at once.

Serves 4

Orange Segments in Red Wine Syrup

Pumpkin and Pecan Ice Cream

8 egg yolks

185g (6oz) caster sugar

375g (12oz) cooked pumpkin, mashed

375ml (12fl oz) double cream, whipped

1 tspn vanilla essence

1 tspn ground cinnamon

1/2 tspn grated nutmeg

125g (4oz) pecan nuts, chopped

1 Beat the egg yolks with the sugar in a bowl until thick and pale. Fold in the remaining ingredients, except the nuts. Pour into a loaf tin, cover with foil; freeze until partially set.

2 Remove the mixture from the freezer and tip it into a large bowl. Beat with an electric hand-held mixer until the ice crystals have broken up. Return to the loaf tin and partially freeze again. Beat the ice cream as before, this time stirring in the pecans.

3 Freeze until firm. Soften in the refrigerator before serving.

Serves 8

Blueberry Champagne Sorbet

375g (12oz) caster sugar

250ml (8fl oz) champagne

500ml (16fl oz) water

500g (1lb) blueberries

125ml (4fl oz) lemon juice

2 egg whites

1 Combine the sugar, champagne and water in a large saucepan. Bring to the boil, lower the heat and simmer for 10 minutes.

2 Blend or process blueberries with lemon juice until smooth. Add to syrup, mix well, then cool to room temperature.

3 Pour mixture into a freezerproof container. Cover and freeze until partially set. Remove from the freezer and break up ice crystals with a fork.

4 Beat egg whites in a grease-free bowl until soft peaks form; fold into the blueberry mixture. Freeze until firm.

Serves 8

Lemon Sorbet with Raspberry Purée

250ml (8fl oz) lemon juice

185g (6oz) caster sugar

1 tblspn finely grated lemon rind

1 litre (13/4pt) water

250ml (8fl oz) lemonade

250g (8oz) raspberries

1 tblspn raspberry jam

1 tblspn raspberry liqueur

1 Combine the lemon juice, sugar and lemon rind in a medium saucepan. Add 125ml (4fl oz) of the water. Stir over moderate heat until the sugar has dissolved; remove from the heat.

2 Stir in the rest of the water and the lemonade. Pour the mixture into a freezerproof container, cover and freeze for 3 hours or until partially set.

3 Remove the sorbet from the freezer and break up the ice crystals with a fork. Return the sorbet to the freezer until firm.

4 Blend or process raspberries with the jam and liqueur until smooth. Press through a sieve into a bowl to remove the seeds. Serve the sauce with the sorbet.

Serves 4

Serving Suggestions

Serve the Lemon Sorbet with Raspberry Purée with a sprig of young mint and two orange or lemon quarters; decorate the Pumpkin and Pecan Ice Cream with chopped pecans and offset the deep burgundy colour of the Blueberry and Champagne Sorbet with a sprig of apple mint.

Lemon Sorbet with Raspberry Purée

Blueberry Champagne Sorbet, Pumpkin and Pecan Ice Cream

Blackcurrant Ripple Ice Cream

| 90g (3oz) caster sugar |
| 125ml (4fl oz) water |
| 250g (8oz) blackcurrants, fresh or frozen |

Ice Cream

| 375ml (12fl oz) double cream |
| 375ml (12fl oz) milk |
| 185g (6oz) sugar |
| 1 tspn vanilla essence |

1 Combine the sugar and half the measured water in a small saucepan. Bring to the boil, stirring, then set aside to cool. In a second saucepan, combine the blackcurrants with the remaining water. Bring to the boil, then lower the heat and simmer for about 20 minutes, stirring frequently, until the blackcurrants soften and the mixture thickens.

2 Mix syrup and blackcurrants in a blender or food processor. Process to a smooth purée. Scrape into a bowl, cover and refrigerate.

3 Make the ice cream. Mix cream, milk, sugar and vanilla essence in a saucepan. Heat to simmering point, stirring until the sugar has dissolved. Pour into a bowl, cover and cool to room temperature, then chill in the refrigerator.

4 Freeze the cream mixture in a freezerproof container until crystals form around the edges; beat until smooth, then freeze again. Alternatively freeze in an ice-cream maker until the mixture reaches a soft-serve consistency.

5 Spoon ice cream and blackcurrant mixture alternately into a glass bowl, forming about six layers.

6 To achieve ripple effect, press down on the dessert, from the surface to the bottom of the bowl, with a spoon. Cover and freeze overnight. To serve, soften the ice cream in the refrigerator for 15 minutes.

Serves 8

Pear and Peach Champagne Sorbet

Two Berry Fruit Salad

| 500g (1lb) raspberries |
| 3 tblspn raspberry liqueur |
| 1 tblspn icing sugar or to taste |
| 500g (1lb) strawberries, hulled, halved if large |
| clotted cream and shortbread fingers to serve |

1 Purée the raspberries with the raspberry liqueur in a blender or food processor. Press through a sieve into a bowl. Stir in icing sugar to taste. Cover the bowl and chill.

2 Divide the strawberries between six dessert plates. Spoon the raspberry purée over each portion.

3 Serve with clotted cream and shortbread.

Serves 6

Pear and Peach Champagne Sorbet

| 375g (12oz) drained canned pears, chopped |
| 375g (12oz) drained canned peaches, chopped |
| 125g (4oz) sugar |
| 155ml (5fl oz) champagne |

1 Process the fruit in a blender or food processor until smooth.

2 Combine sugar and champagne in a large saucepan. Simmer gently until sugar has dissolved.

3 Stir in puréed fruit. When cool, pour mixture into a freezerproof container. Cover and freeze for 3 hours or until partially set.

4 Remove sorbet from freezer and break up ice crystals with a fork. Return sorbet to freezer until firm. Serve in scoops, decorated with strips of lime rind if liked.

Serves 6

Useful Information

Length

Centimetres	Inches	Centimetres	Inches
0.5 (5mm)	$1/4$	18	7
1	$1/2$	20	8
2	$3/4$	23	9
2.5	1	25	10
4	$1^1/2$	30	12
5	2	35	14
6	$2^1/2$	40	16
7.5	3	45	18
10	4	50	20
15	6	NB: 1cm = 10mm	

Metric/Imperial Conversion Chart
Mass (Weight)
(Approximate conversions for cookery purposes)

Metric	Imperial	Metric	Imperial
15g	$1/2$oz	315g	10oz
30g	1oz	350g	11oz
60g	2oz	375g	12oz ($3/4$lb)
90g	3oz	410g	13oz
125g	4oz ($1/4$lb)	440g	14oz
155g	5oz	470g	15oz
185g	6oz	500g (0.5kg)	16oz (1lb)
220g	7oz	750g	24oz ($1^1/2$lb)
250g	8oz ($1/2$lb)	1000g (1kg)	32oz (2lb)
280g	9oz	1500 (1.5kg)	3lb

Metric Spoon Sizes

$1/4$ teaspoon	= 1.25ml
$1/2$ teaspoon	= 2.5ml
1 teaspoon	= 5ml
1 tablespoon	=15ml

Liquids

Metric	Imperial
30ml	1fl oz
60ml	2fl oz
90ml	3fl oz
125ml	4fl oz
155ml	5fl oz ($1/4$pt)
185ml	6fl oz
250ml	8fl oz
500ml	16fl oz
600ml	20fl oz (1pt)
750ml	$1^1/4$pt
1 litre	$1^3/4$pt
1.2 litres	2pt
1.5 litres	$2^1/2$pt
1.8 litres	3pt
2 litres	$3^1/2$pt
2.5 litres	4pt

Index

Editorial Coordination: Merehurst Limited
Cookery Editor: Jenni Fleetwood
Editorial Assistant: Sheridan Packer
Production Managers: Sheridan Carter, Anna Maguire
Layout and Finished Art: Stephen Joseph
Cover Photography: David Gill
Cover Design: Maggie Aldred
Cover Home Economist: Liz Trigg
Cover Stylist: Hilary Guy

Published by J.B. Fairfax Press Pty Limited
80-82 McLachlan Avenue
Rushcutters Bay, NSW 2011
A.C.N. 003 738 430

Formatted by J.B. Fairfax Press Pty Limited
Printed by Toppan Printing Co, Singapore

JBFP 317 A/UK
Includes Index
ISBN 1 86343 116 0 (set)
ISBN 1 86343 156 X

Distribution and Sales Enquiries
Australia: J.B. Fairfax Press Pty Limited
Ph: (02) 361 6366 Fax: (02) 360 6262
United Kingdom: J.B. Fairfax Press Limited
Ph: (0933) 402330 Fax: (0933) 402234